Poetic Life Experiences

Tabitha Edwards-Walton

Energion Publications
Gonzalez, FL
2015

Copyright © 2015, Tabitha Edwards-Walton

Cover Design: Tabitha Edwards-Walton & Henry Neufeld

Cover Image: © Rolffimages | Dreamstime.com - Surreal Time Spiral Photo

ISBN10: 1-63199-177-6
ISBN13: 978-1-63199-177-9
Library of Congress Control Number: 2015941854

Energion Publications
P. O. Box 841
Gonzalez, FL 32560

energion.com
pubs@energion.com
850-525-3916

Dedication

I would like to give a special thanks to a special man in my life,
my dad.
Dad, you have taught me so many things,
such as it always pays to be a hard worker.
You have taught me the value of love.
And the most important thing you taught me in my life
was the importance of family.
I love you so much, Dad.

Acknowledgments

A special thank you to Deanna, Ray, Ashley, Anastasia (Lily), Astrid, my parents (Keith and Regina), and Henry and Jody Neufeld at Energion Publications.

Rebeca Enos, Hazel Harper, Debbie Trent, and God, without the love and support of these I would not have been able to do this. They believed in me. They let me know that my words were worth enough to put into a book, or they inspired me in some special way.

Table of Contents

Dedication iii
Acknowledgments iv
Introduction vii

Life is about Time, Patience and Balance 1
Depression 2
Love that is No More 3
Life Experience 4
The Last Breath of Air 5
My Hero 6
The Fallen Soldier 8
One Life Taken, One Life Born 9
The Day He Has Waited For 11
This is Really What is Best For You 12
You Are Not My Mom 13
A Mother's Self-Blame 15
Living life with Attention Deficit Hyper Activity Disorder 16
Moonlit Stroll with a Perfect Gentleman 17
The Empty Nest 18
The day I heard the news! 19
Memories from the Past 20
Alzheimer's Took Her from Me! 21
The Bittersweet Departure 23
A Man's Last Cry 24
Divorce 25
Eyes of a Weeping Willow 26
September Days 27
The Release 29

The Note That was Left Behind	30
Mama's Voice	31
Control or Lost Soul	32
Night Prowler	33
Life Coach	34
Life Really Can Be a Bed of Roses	35
The Uniform of the Law	36
The Engulfed Carroty Blaze	37
September 11	39
I Wear Pink for You	40
North Bound Railroad	42
North and South	43
"The Headless Horseman" Review	45
To Reduce Life's Stress and Anxieties	46
Quiet the Mind, Quiet the Body	47
The Healing Bridge	48
True Testament of Love at First Sight	49
Dancing in the Mist	50

Introduction

Writing this book I had my own life experiences:

I started a new job.

I legally got married to my lover even though we had previously been married in a different country for 11 years. We were allow to be married in the United States in front of our friends and family.

My daughter and my grandchildren moved from three hours away to nearly twenty-five hours away.

I found that I absolutely love the arts more than I thought. I went to a couple of ballets. My son and I went to an art museum.

I would not have been able to write this book if it was not for music. I listen to endless hours of music. There were days it was just me and music. I would put head phones on and type to the sound of the songs that played. The music inspired me to write. Towards the end of this book, I found that I loved instrumental music better then music with a voice. The soft piano type. I found I would type to the beat of the music. I would close my eyes and if I had word block, the words would just pour out like I was a new profound composer or something. My computer keys became like a piano. The words came to me as the music came to Mozart or Bach. Tracy Chapman got me through the first half of the book and The Piano Guys got me through the second half. Remember:

> Poetry is emotions
> coming from the mind and the heart
> that can be written and spoken.
>
> – Tabitha

Calm the palpating heart,
the racing thoughts;
quiet the mind,
and love yourself to enjoy life to the fullest.

–Tabitha Edwards-Walton.

Life is about Time, Patience and Balance

"Live life in the moment, for it is always the right time!"

"One can do anything with enough patience."

"Even the slightest movement can knock one off balance."

Depression

Depression affects many across our country.
For some, it is only a small fraction of their lives.
For others, it consumes their complete identity.
Depression forces some to leave behind husbands or wives.

It gets too be much for one to bare.
So his or her on life, he or she does take.
Depression then hurts the ones left behind that love and care.
What a tragedy this does make.

Depression got the better of one man today.
This man made everyone laugh for years.
To ease his family's pain, I do pray,
For I know they must be heart broke and in tears.

Not many could make people laugh like you do!
Your movies and comedy will live forever.
Robin Williams, many will miss you,
But you will continue give us your laughter.

Love That is No More

My identity is slowly fading.
My tears are now cascading.
My body is falling, crawling and trying to stand.
I am begging and pleading for your hand.

Your heart no longer feels the same.
You think this is now a game.
You turn back to see this as a pathetic plea.
You are trying to move on; you want nothing more to do with me.

I am now a mere puddle on the floor.
You are only steps away from actually walking out the door.
You are leaving me; you are walking out of my life.
This pain I am now feeling is cutting me like a knife.

I crawl to my feet, "Baby, without you how will I breathe?"
You say, "Know I am doing this because I do still love you,"
as you lie through your teeth.
I cannot turn off my love like it is a light switch.
Without your love I might as well dig my own ditch.

Life Experience

Life as we know it starts with the first breath we take.
It also expires with the last breath that we breathe.
Some may have a wonderful life, others experience a life full of heartache.
We only have one life, but it does not have to be the one we are stuck with.

Each of us have different experiences in the life we live.
For each of us our lives bring about different trails.
Some will make their existence very effective.
While others will have some epic fails.

Some people will encounter events that are out of their control.
While others will be in complete control, but will make poor choices.
Some people will have wonderful souls,
Yet, there will be some who are just savages.

Life will happen for each of us. Until Death.
One can roll with it, or one can take a different path.
One can end it, by taking away their very own breath.
The human species is capable of love, or to live a life in wrath.

The Last Breath of Air

I am now with my last existence at the edge.
I am no longer thinking about my future.
For there is nothing left for me! That is why I am out here on this very ledge.
I have been told all my life that I was a born loser.

I do not think about or look at the darkness that I know is below.
I am now taking a moment to reflect on the past twenty-five years.
I have already done as much destruction as I can,
it is now okay if I push off and let the rest of myself go.
When people hear the news of my crumbled body,
there will not be any sadness or any tears.

I will not dare ask for God's forgiveness,
as am about to I dive into the obscure darkness.
I will not beg him to save my soul.
I am a person who feels nothing, I am completely emotionless.
I am just wasted space on a census poll.

I am leaning forward, pushing off with my toes and down goes my head.
Now to take my very last breath of air.
The next time anyone sees my mutilated body, I will be dead.
People will gasp, people will say who was this? But no one will really care.

My Hero

He left his life of nothing behind him,
    when he walked into the military recruiting office.
He was only seventeen years old.
    He walked away from his family. It was his decision.
He went onto boot camp, then he went to active service.
He was then a Marine. He was flown to Vietnam,
    which was all the way across the ocean.
It was such an honor for him, that he served his country.
Oh, how he missed his family!
    He knew this is what God had called for him to do.
Out in the battlefields,
    even the worst guy in the unit was still his buddy.
He did everything he could to make sure everyone was safe.
    Although they lost a few.

He came home from the war, not a scratch on him,
    he was lucky he was alive.
He was never home long before he had to leave again.
This job was not your typical nine to five.
That is how it was for the military back then.

One time on leave he met a girl, they got married.
They were not married for long before he had to go to Germany.
When she finally got there,
    that is when he found out that she was large-bellied.
She was pregnant with his first baby.

By this time he had transferred out of the Marines
        and into the Army.
He continued to move around every couple of years
He felt it was his civic duty.
He was a man of no fears.

He volunteered to go back to Vietnam for a second tour.
This time around he saved more lives.
        He dragged a high ranking officer to a fox hole,
while bullets flew all around.
        He thought he would be dead for sure.
He lived, unscratched, because he did not lose control.
Two children later and a twenty year career.
I am proud of who he was. He retired from the US. Army.
This man is still with us today. He is still here.
This man is my hero. Thank you, Daddy.

The Fallen Soldier

I look to the left where your loving body once lay.
I run my hand across the pillow that used to caress your hair.
I am so lost without you, for your life is now gone.
    I can only remember our times of yesterday.
I was not ready to be alone.
    I won't be able to manage during this time of despair.

I still have dreams about you and that horrible night.
The night when they knocked upon my door to notify me of your death.
They handed me your Purple Heart medal,
    and said your body would soon be in flight.
I still recall, I screamed so loudly, as I collapsed to the floor, gasping for my breath.

We had vowed that together we would grow old.
You went off to war, but you got too close to the line of fire.
I was left without your tender lips to kiss or soft hand to hold.
I was left without my heart's desire.

You were my husband and you were a mighty soldier.
Thank you for your service, sorry your life ended so abruptly.
You were a hero in my eyes before you died, but that is sure to be carried over.
You did your duties as you said you would do. I honored you and you have honored our Country.

One Life Taken, One Life Born

Her scrubs are neat, her stethoscope around her neck.
She never knew what the day would bring; she was ready.
She heard over the intercom, that there has been a bad wreck.
She did not pay much attention, initially.

For she worked in a different part of the hospital.
So she went on tending to her patients.
Then she heard the page for Nurse Campbell.
She swiftly moved through the departments.

She arrived in the Emergency room, fully willing to assist.
Little did she know, it was her own son?
Her breath caught, she wanted to turn. This image she wanted to dismiss.
She then took over his primary care, she no longer wanted to run.

She tried so hard to be strong for her son. She fought back the tears.
His body was in pieces it had been shattered and torn.
Frantically she tried to save his life, she heard the sounds she often hears.
It was the sounds of lullaby, this means that a new life had been born.
She and the others did all that they could.
Right there in their hands, her son died.
That day she lost her only son, her young man.
    She knew she had to do something good.
She decided to donate his organs, including his eyes.
    This would have completed his pride.

The baby born that day was unable to see,
She gave this child the gift of her son's corneas.
Of course she was told there was no guarantee
The child was indeed able to see perfect images.

Nurse Campbell met the family of the child.
She became the child's God parent.
When she was with this special person, she smiled.
This child brought back memories of that horrible accident.

However Nurse Campbell was never saddened.
Through this adorable child, she got to see her son's eyes.
They were filled with passion and very determined.
Oh how they sparkled like the diamonds in the skies.

The Day He Has Waited For

The doctor lay his newborn child in his arms for him to hold.
He had waited for this moment for a very long time.
    His daughter was finally here.
He looked down at his this new life in his arms.
    He felt like he was going to pass out cold.
His body turned into a ball of emotions, His eyes were filled with so much moisture that it came out as a one big tear.
He talked to her for nine months, now he just stood there in awe.
She was so beautiful.
He thought to himself, *"She is our formation, she is our design."*
He was finally able to stutter, "Hi, sweetie, I am your Pa."
He looked to his wife, he managed to choke out the words,
    "She is healthy, and perfectly fine."

He looked back down to his daughter and he said to her,
    "I promise to you that I will always be there for you."
The saline rolled down from his eyes and baptized her head.
    He pulled her close to his heart.
Then he said this to her, "No matter what life throws at you,
    we will work together to get through.
I am your dad, I will always love you no matter what,
    even if you move away or if we are ever apart."

As soon as he handed his daughter to his wife,
    he no longer was able to stand, He fell to his knees.
He placed his hands together, as he bowed his head.
He was one with the floor,
    Thanking God for special moments like these.
The hospital staff stood silent and weepy eyed,
    at the end of the new family's bed.

This is Really What is Best For You

The hardest thing I had to do in my life was to walk away.
I knew I could not give you want you needed.
I could not provide for you, not the way you needed me to.
I hope I will see your face again one day.

Please do not hate me, for what I have done.
Believe me when I say, I did it because I love you.
It was so hard, I cried every day.
I did it because I wanted you to have so much more, Son.

Yes, I gave birth to you. I am sure you do not understand,
Why a mother can let someone else raise her baby.
I did not have the tools, knowledge or resources,
To make you into a better man.

You have my blood that runs through your veins, this is true.
I have come from a hard complicated life, I have done so much.
I struggle daily to keep myself alive.
If I would have kept you with me
      that would not have been good for you.

I hope one day that you are able to forgive me.
I do not ask that you love me.
I also hope that your family is good to you.
I wish you to be as happy as you can be.

You Are Not My Mom

She was taken from her mom when she was just 3 years old.
From that time she had been shifted from home to home.
She was taken because there was no food and the house was too cold.

Her hair was a mess, through it they could not even get a comb.
She was dirty, and bruised.
The state came to remove her to take her to a new place.
They pulled her from her mom's arms, this left her hurt and confused.
From that point on, she became just another one of their children,
    a number on a case.

She did not want to love, she did not want to get close,
    and she lived her life in fear.
Just when she started to get settled, she had to move again.
This was the third home this dear girl had to endure that year.
She knew it would be repeated, she just didn't know where or when.

Her foster families would say that she was just too mean.
They would say that she did not do well in school.
They would say that everywhere they took her she would cause a scene.
They would question, why did she have to break every single rule?

They tried to show her acceptance and love.
They tried to guide her in the right directions.
But she just pushed them away. And did things they were not proud of.
She rejected all their affections.

She blamed herself for being taken away.
She built up some tough walls,
After she was taken from her mom's arms that day.
The pain just continued because her mom never continued the calls.

The one love she truly yearned for was the love of her mother.
No one ever understood, what this little girl was going through.
They just tried to replace her mom with another.
This left her afraid to get close to anyone and she always felt blue.

She was afraid that if she was to love again, she would be forced apart.
She would act out so that she would not have to stay.
Because she did not want to show them just how much this hurt her heart.
What she secretly wanted was someone who could love her unconditionally.
She knew she would find this one love again one day.

The years passed, the families came and went.
This girl continued to misbehave.
In foster care is where her childhood years were spent.
Some did not think that she was worth the save.

So many gave up on her.
Then one day they placed her with a family
      that was very loving and supporting.
They treated her like she was their own daughter.
She started loving, her life turned around, she finally stopped hurting.

A Mother's Self-Blame

I sat there and I wondered where things went wrong
I have failed as a parent! I have tried to do things right.
What is the length of time that she has felt like this? - How long?
According to these writings I found it didn't just happen overnight.

I should have known, I should have seen the signs.
She is my baby. Why didn't I know?
Why is it that I had to find out like this? Hidden in poetic lines.
She is my daughter, but these days she barely even takes the time to say hello.

I wanted it to be just a phase she was going through.
Did I make her this way? I know she has always been a tom boy
       since she was a little girl!
God, please tell me this was not the case. That It was not true.
I know this is her life, but this kind of news
       at first made my thoughts spin and twirl.

Did I not spend enough time with her showing her how to be feminine?
Did I not teach her the right way to love a man?
Was I blind and naive? Did I not pay her enough attention?
I knew I had to talk to her about this, but I had no ideas or a plan.

One night I just asked her if we could go out to shop.
She accepted. During the ride, there was a bunch of silence.
When we got to where we wanted to be, when the car came to a stop,
I looked to her and she looked back to me.
    I said, "Over the years I know we have had our distance.

You know you can talk to me about anything, right?
I found your writings, I want you to know I now understand."
The tears in both our eyes started to fall. Keeping them in was a fight.
I looked my daughter in the eyes and I took her by the hand.

Living Life with Attention Deficit Hyper Activity Disorder

Living life with Attention Deficit Hyper Activity Disorder,
Is a constant struggle for the child and the parent.
The child is always full of energy
      and the parent always seems to be fatigued.
Finding the right balance is a tall order.

Just remember, it is like a circus inside the child's mind.
There are so many thoughts going on.
The child has little to no impulse control.
The parent has to try to remain loving and kind.

The child cannot sit still without the aid of medication.
The child excessively talks about what they think.
The parents wish for just a few moment of silence.
They both feel the frustration.

The ADHD child does not require much sleep.
The child just cannot turn off the thoughts in his mind.
This leaves the parents physically exhausted.
Sometimes it is hard not to just sit and weep.

One must remember that this is a disease.
The child cannot control the behaviors and thoughts.
By being a patient and loving parent,
You will get through moments like these!

Moonlit Stroll with a Perfect Gentleman

You were dressed for success.
You had on a brand new black beret,
A well groomed dress shirt, your tie was perfectly tied.
Pants that were pressed so sharp they were crisp,
polished shoes, and you were dressed to impress.

You wanted the room to notice you for you. Not your disabilities.
You did not have a care at all that you could not stand long.
It did not bother you that you did not know how to read the script.
You just did your thing, you smiled at everyone especially the ladies.

You did not even know we were going. It was not rehearsed.
You just got up there and had the time of your life.
I told you one of the lines and you got it right off. As I knew you would.
They did not have you repeat many lines, but you did not even care.
It did not matter to you if you were not picked to go first.

You did not want me to help you at all on this night.
You were determined to show just how independent you were.
For a disabled ten year old who wanted nothing more than to be normal,
In my eyes you shined like a star, you were a divine delight.

As we walked out you took my hand to escort me.
You said, "Let me carry your purse, I want to be the perfect gentleman!"
As far as I am concerned you already are.
I am so proud of the young man you have turned out to be.

We walked across the street, you were concerned I might get hit.
I assured you I was fine. We strolled under the moon in the grass.
We held hands, I had the thought of how perfect my life was,
Because I have this perfect gentleman in it.

The Empty Nest

Now that you are grown, and it is time for you to leave,
How on Earth will I handle the emptiness?
I am sad, you are now longer a little child,
I know you have your life ahead of you to achieve.

Some facts will never change. I will always be your Mother.
Just because you are moving out on your own,
Please pick up the phone, or come over often.
This does not mean you have to be a stranger.

I know I will suffer from the empty nest.
I will worry for a while when you do not come home.
I will probably call you and say, "Where are you?
Are you safe?" You will say, "Mom, give it a rest!"

I will go through the house and turn on all the lights.
Then I will go and turn them off one by one.
When I come to yours, I know the tears will fall.
I will sadly turn it off, say "I love you," and say "good night."

The day I heard the news!

I wished I could pull the words back off my tongue;
That had already formed in my mouth.
What! You're going to have a baby!
I regretted what I had said, "you are way too young."

Please tell me it is not true!
I wish you would have waited,
Just for a little while longer.
You have your whole life a head of you.

Well the deed is done now. There is nothing else to do.
There is no need to continue to lecture.
For it will not change things, now we have to prepare.
Do you know if we have to buy pink or blue?

The best gift in the world is when your child becomes a parent.
Seeing that new baby for the first time.
The first look at the next generation.
Forever hold onto that very special moment.

Memories from the Past

I looked into the mirror, what before me did I see?
My hair a long ago became grayed.
The wrinkles were prominent and deep.
Memories of my life flashed back at me.

First were the images of a long haired, brown eyed child.
Happy but shy was I.
I was very much a daddy's girl.
Whenever he walked into the room, I would just smile.

Next flashed the images of my teenage years.
This was a time I searched for my own identity.
I did things I was not proud of.
Some were heavily influenced by my peers.

Oh, what a delight, next the years that I became independent.
I went out on my own, I got married. I started own my family.
I tried to be a good wife and a good mom.
I hope showed my kids how to be a good parent.

The reflections in the mirror, was like a slide show.
They brought back so many memories, with each image,
That appeared before me. It was hard to believe, that so many
years have passed. Where did the time go!

The illustrations represented a Life that was very good.
I was not rich with money, but I was rich with love.
I had everything I ever wanted.
It was picture perfect from where I stood.

Alzheimer's Took Her from Me!

When it first started, it was so insignificant that I did not notice.
Mom would forget small things here and there, no big deal.
We as humans all do this from time to time.
It did not mean that she had any form of an illness.

Mom started to forget more and more as time passed.
I thought to myself, this was just a normal process as she aged.
She would miss place items that she just had.
I was naive to think it would not progress or last.

Mom quickly started having a hard time recalling people
        she had known for years.
She even forgot where she went to high school.
Mom forgot to pay her own bills. Mom's cognition was fading.
 I had to face facts. I no longer could let this fall on my deaf ears.

It did not take her long, before she forgot her own address.
As she struggled daily with her memory.
The ability to take care of herself started to decrease.
She required assistance to go shopping or to properly dress.

The sweet woman I have known all my life, had become combative.
She no longer recognized me by my face, she didn't even know my name.
She would spout out mean, hateful words' I know she did not mean them.
Alzheimer's disease took my mom and left me
        with someone that was fragile and defensive.

The doctors keep her in a medicated sedative state.
She was no longer able to care for herself.
There were days she no longer remembered how to eat.
Her life reduced to not being able to hold her own head up straight.

If I could give her one gift. I would give just one memory
I would let her remember what it feels like to be loved.
I would let her feel the love that we have never lost for her.
I would let her bask in the unconditional beauty.

The Bittersweet Departure

The elderly woman weakened and frail lay in her bed.
The cancer is accelerating her mortality.
Her husband of seventy years holds her hand and strokes her head.
She looks to him, and starts to whisper. He listens intently.

As I lay here, I am reflecting back on my life,
Together, we have been through so much.
For so many years, we have been husband and wife.
To this day, I still love feeling your warm soft touch.

You have fulfilled my every desire.
You have been my heart and soul.
You have been my foundation, and my empire.
You are my completeness, you are my whole.

The time has come my dear!
Please take care of things, you have some obligations to fill.
She reaches and wipes away his falling tear.
She musters the words, "I love you, I always have and I always will!"

She closes her eyes as she takes her last breath.
Her heart stops beating.
The elderly man now knows that the love of his life has gently embraced death.
He weeps for a while but he knows in Heaven they will again be meeting.

A Man's Last Cry

An elderly man whose wife had just passed, and left him all alone,
He had so many things to do, he had so many people to call.
He sat shaken and disturbed, he clumsily tried to reach for the phone.
Heart broken, His aged memory searched for the numbers to recall.

Tears drenching his cheeks, they fell slowly down to his shirt,
Finally they dripped to the floor.
He anticipated his love to expire, it did not stop the hurt.
They had been together since he was – twenty-four.

She was all that this man had known, it truly was love at first sight.
She was his rock and he her empire.
He said out loud, "How on Earth am I going to make it without her tonight?"
"She is all that I am, she is all that I desire."

This elderly man continued to try and carry out his life for a while.
The pain got too much to bear.
His heart ached for his love so much he had to force himself to smile.
"God, please forgive me for what I am about to do," he whispered in a prayer.

The elderly man now looked up towards the Heavenly sky.
"I am sorry my dearest, I know you are watching up above,"
this man cried his last cry.
"I love you, I always have and I always will, my love."

Divorce

When two people entered into a marriage,
They took a vow of commitment.
This should have been a give and take relationship.
It should not have been where one was made to feel like garbage.

Once the marriage license was signed.
One or both of the people began to change.
The feelings were no longer the same.
The love they once felt was no longer combined.

The expectations were not what one thought.
Sometimes one or the other had a wondering eye.
Some found that there was just simply not enough time.
This led them to stray after they had fought.

Some had regrets about getting married.
    They verbally attacked each other with fullforce.
Sometimes this left them hurt and with feelings of betrayal.
Very few couples were actually able to remain friends,
Once their marriage ended in divorce.
The divorce rate is so much higher these days.
People do not take the time to make their marriages work.
Some rush in and rush out.
Some people are not willing to change their ways.

People do not realize the impact
    that divorce may have on someone's life.
Did those two people really put in the full effort?
When that commitment was made to each other,
They made a vow to be husband and wife.

Eyes of a Weeping Willow

Tears stained my pillow,
As I cried over your loss.
The pain was so deep,
My eyes drooped like a weeping willow.

I lost, my best friend, my companion.
Your life will never be forgotten.
The ache in my heart will never be healed.
I await the day I will see you in Heaven.

You could not tell him "No!"
He called upon you.
It was your time.
You had to go!

Time is something I wished I had more of.
I still wanted to be with you.
I would have held you longer.
It was hard to say good-bye, My Love.

September Days

For many of us, September Days means summer is almost over,
the season will soon change to fall.
The animals are starting to prepare to hibernate. They are organizing to take cover.
The main sport of the season is now football.

This means that the leaves are about do some modifications.
The weather is starting to turn colder.
There might even be snow upon the caps of the mountains.
People may be chopping more firewood, stacking it higher and higher.
For some people September is full of emotions.

For one special couple this very month is very hard for them.
They struggle just to get through the days that many of us take for granted.
God decided this was the month, that he need one more angel to join Him.
This is the very month that their angel's life ended.

When everyone's colors become bright – theirs are graying and dark.
When everyone's days are just starting to get cooler – Theirs are so much colder.
They are not able to watch his children play at the park.
They did not have the pleasure to watch him grow older.

They had questioned God at the time of James' Death.
They wondered why this had to happen to them.
It almost took away their very own breath.
They realized they had a purpose – they were not being condemned.

Even though this time of year is very rough
They still manage to put their focus forward.
They still see the animals and the vibrant colors through the windows.
They embrace the cold, because they are both
warm of heart, even though it is very tough.
So please think of them the next time you see the September leaves
starting to turn to the reds and yellows.

The Birth of Jesus Christ

On a night a long time ago, a poor couple gave life
to a special child.
People traveled from all over to see this tiny baby.
They brought gifts to give to this newly born boy.
He just laid there, he looked up and smiled.

He was born under the brightest star in a manger.
He was not concerned who came to see him.
He did not worry if one had a gift or not.
He did not care if one were a King or a farmer.

Upon the hay he happily laid
Surrounded by his parents and the animals.
Encircled around them were his many visitors.
This is how the Nativity scene was first displayed.

Setting up a nativity display is still around for some this very day.
Some people go to church to celebrate the birth Jesus Christ.
Some people gather to eat a meal together.
Others gather around with family
to allow their children to run and play.

Jesus allows us to celebrate his birthday every year.
It is a time for joy and happiness.
Some exchange gifts with each other.
Sometimes the meaning of this day gets lost or may disappear.

The Son of God is the reason
To decorate with Holiday Lights.
To give or to get presents.
Or to celebrate this and every Holiday Season.

The Release

Hidden beneath the cloak of clothing, I bear the scars,
That were put there to release the thoughts that were inside.
The wounds are jagged but now healed. They are not perfect lined bars.
And it was not so much the marks on my skin that I tried to hide.

It was the emotions that I did not let anyone see.
When I held a sharp object to the taut skin,
It was to discharge the ill fillings to set them free.
It was not because I wanted to die, It was so I could live life fully again.

One day the knife went in too deep.
I lost a lot of blood, I was found on the floor.
My mom thought I was dead, but I was just asleep.
She thought I tried to commit Suicide at twenty-four.

She rushed me to the hospital, there I stayed,
For three full days. They found out I was not suicidal.
I was just full of emotional pain, and afraid.
I thought cutting to release was acceptable.

I found someone to help liberate me from the feelings.
I no longer held it all in.
I learned to talk to my therapist at our meetings.
After that episode I never put a piercing object to my skin.

The Note That was Left Behind

He walked right in to the school like he did every other day.
Today he wore all black; he sat and he waited.
When he felt the time was right, he pulled out his knife.
Later they found a note. It read: let me tell you when my life went astray.

Little do you all know, but both of my parents are sick in the head.
They loved me unconditionally in front of others.
From the time I was a small child they would come to my room,
In the shadows of the darkness, and do horrible things to me in my bed.

I was always forced to wear a smile.
I had to pretend like we were a perfect family.
I cannot handle their sadistic madness any more.
Today, I ended my misery, I made it worth my while.

I awoke early to find them both asleep.
I made them suffer but not in the same way,
That I have endured for years.
Now it is time for me to kill myself because I am in 'way too deep.

I am sure you are asking why the school?
This is because this is the only place I truly felt safe.
I am sorry I made a mess.
I am sorry that for all these years I have been the fool.

The class president's body was found in the bathroom
His bloody wrist split wide open.
Everyone thought he had the perfect life.
So be careful what you assume.

Mama's Voice

You think you are so big and so tough,
Because you are livin' your life hangin' with street gang thugs.
You all are making life for the rest of communities very rough.
It means nothing to you to shoot your guns in the streets
or to push your harmful drugs.

The gang's leader tells you that a rival gang member is in your part of town.
He tells you, "to shoot him dead."
He says if you get caught "I won't let you go down."
Please child, learn that these people don't care about you,
they are just messin' with your head!

You are fortunate, so far you are eluding the law.
You are dodging bullets. How long will you be able to stay safe?
I don't want you to end up in jail or dead because you drew the short straw.
I beg you just walk away! Make yourself a waif.

You are so young, make something good out of your life.
Get out before it is too late, Get out of this gang. Make a better choice.
Get a nice job, Have a good family, and be a good husband to your wife.
I say again," Please, child, listen to your Mama's lovin' voice."

Control or Lost Soul

I am robber, I am a cheater.
I am indeed a thief.
I make my own decisions, I am my own keeper.
I cause pain, I make life full of grief.

I burn many bridges.
So that there is no visible trace.
I leave people with broken hearts and yearning wishes.
I deprive loved ones of the smiles they wear upon their face.

I divert all attention from you to me.
You see, this is the easiest thing to do.
All I have to do is make someone feel euphoric for just a moment,
the grip you thought you had on them is now free!
Then from you, they are free!

In case you cannot figure it out, I am the addictions that take over others' lives.
Once I gain control, there will not be much that anyone could do.
It does not matter, I am a predator.
I go after your kids, your husbands, and even your wives.
You never know, my next victim might just be you!

Once I am in charge there is only one way for someone to regain control.
They have to live again, they have to be willing to fight.
If not, I will consume their entire being, I will become their soul.
It has to be something that they really want.
They will know exactly when to do it. When the time is right.

Night Prowler

He drives around for hours hidden
behind the dark-tinted windows of his car.
He stays just out of sight.
He watches his beauty from afar.
He carefully stalks his pray at night.

He waits until he knows she is alone.
He lurks around in the darkness, where no one else can see.
He disconnects the telephone.
He sneaks in and locks the door behind him,
he doesn't want her to flee.

He does not want to take her life.
He just wants to take what he thinks is his.
He walks to her bed and to her throat he holds his knife.
He tells her, "Do Not Fight. You now belong to me.
That is the way it is!"

She says to him, "I know who you are.
While you were watching me, I was watching you."
She looks him square in the eyes and says, "Isn't that bizarre!
Now you are under arrest! Which is long overdue."

Life Coach

We have spent hours sitting across from each other.
At first it was so hard for me to communicate.
So, I could pour out my heart, my soul and my thoughts.
Learning to relax was something that I had to discover.

You were very patient, you always had a relaxed calming demeanor.
You knew how to break the ice, you knew the topics to avoid.
You always knew how to make me relax;
      I did not even know you were accomplishing it,
Especially if I was extremely upset or overflowing with anger.

Talking to you always made me feel comfortable.
There were many times I forgot you were even in the room.
I often thought I was talking to myself.
I thought I was out on a trail surrounded by nature.
I would forget that you were there to help me as a professional.

At the point I started seeing you, my life was spinning out of harmony.
You helped me regain my focus and direction.
You facilitated me to find the tools I needed to keep my balance.
You helped me center myself in finding my own gravity.

Thank you for making those hours available for me.
I know there were days where I just rambled.
You compassionately listened, without bother.
You allowed the emotions inside of me to be set free.

I still have moments where my life loses that stability.
I know I can turn to you as my Life Coach for guidance.
Life is more than just a year long. You have no problem letting me talk.
I know this is not something that you would just do for everybody.

Life Really Can Be A Bed of Roses

"Life is a bed of roses," this of course is a cliché.
It all depends on how one chooses to use this phrase.
Roses can be full of painful thorns,
    or they can be stunningly beautiful.
Roses are like life; it depends on one's perception or how they lay.

Life as it compares to roses, both require certain basic elements
to allow them survive.
They both need proper food and hydration.
They both need attention and devotion.
Just receiving these basics, will allow them to remain alive.

To gain a life that can even compare to the beautiful bed of roses,
There is so much that one must accomplish.
One must love thyself.
    Then the outer beauty will glimmer from inside out.
One must be mindful of certain influences.

These influences can turn one's life into the rose's thorn.
They can be around at any given time, they can be in any form.
They can leave one bleeding and hurt,
    they can cause a life to wither.
They can leave one looking tired and worn.

It is up to you to choose if you want your life to be wonderful
like the petals of the rose.
It could be bright and full of different colors.
It could be smooth like petals made of silk.
The bloom of fullness would be sure to show.

The Uniform of the Law

For the men and women who wear the uniform of the law:
You each have taken the oath to protect and serve.
Every day you put your own life on the line, to keep ours safe.
Sometimes you do not always get the best luck of the draw.

You drive hours in your cruisers, or walk your beats.
You have to be available in a moment's notice.
You have to be out on the Holidays, in all kinds of weather.
You are the watchful eye on our city streets.

You are usually the first to respond to the scenes.
It does not matter if it is a domestic dispute, a robbery, or an accident.
Most of you are proud to wear that shield upon your uniform.
You actually enjoy your responsibility, your routines.

Some may yell brutality, they do not want to think it was justice.
Some people do not realize how your job could be dangerous.
Some may even say it may have been racially motivated.
Sometimes there is not enough gratitude for your service.

Some people want to harm you instead of honoring you.
Some people disobey your commands,
They may even call you disrespecting names.
To Protect and Serve is what you do, so Thank You!

The Engulfed Carroty Blaze

In the blackness of the night, the alarm in the house blares.
Everyone jumps to their feet. They don on protective clothing.
To the trucks and on the road in minutes.
In route to the scene, everyone in Squad 4 prepares.

The small apartment building is engulfed in a carroty blaze.
A thick obscured smoke rolling from the glassless windows.
People descend from the inferno,
In a state of desperation and smoke inhalation haze.

The trucks are producing a strobe-like affect.
Fire personnel are frantically working, hooking up hoses
To fire trucks and to fire hydrants.
They know they have lives to save and to protect.

Squad 4 rushes through the blackness of the smoke.
They cannot see their hands in front of their faces.
It hard to breath even through their oxygenated masks.
They push on, even though every breath makes them choke.

The heat is so intense, it was burning through their gear.
They trudge forward. They check every room.
They have to make sure that everyone has gotten out.
They will not abandon their positions until this building is clear.

The Captain calls over the radio from outside,
"It appears that a small child is still in there!
You're the only squad that can save his life!
He is only one hundred feet to your right side."

Squad 4 turns to the right, they come to a closed door.
They burst through. To their surprise
This room is clear of fire but filled with smoke.
The little boy lay lifeless on the floor.

One fireman scoops the boy's body up, he removes his mask.
With it he covers the boy's face.
All the firemen of Squad 4 proceeds to exit the burning building.
The little boy lives. They complete their task.

September 11

9-11 is the day many Americans will never forget.
This is the day that our land was invaded,
Many lives were lost, three buildings were hit.
An attack was planned, put into motion,
and was carried out without regret.
Years have passed but this day will never become jaded.

The two twin buildings crumbled, entombing the life of thousands.
This left the world at a loss. We were stunned and mortified.
This all happened in a matter of seconds.
Attacks like this does not happen on our soil, not in our Countryside.

Life for many of us went on after that day
but for thousands it did not.
We went on doing what we normally do.
On the yearly anniversary, we have to let the deceased know
that they were not forgotten,
Even if they were strangers to you!

Every year please take a few moments,
to remember those tragic events of this day.
Try to visit Ground Zero where the Towers once stood,
Or sometime during the exact few hours of the day,
try to stop in silence to pray.
This will really do your heart some good.

I Wear Pink For You

This is for Leona, Melissa, Hazel, Debbie S. and all the other women and men who are lucky enough to be survivors. My heart goes out for the ones that are not. I love you, Barbara Walton, even though I never had the pleasure of meeting you.

I sat nervously in the doctor's office anxious and full of dreaded fear.
When the doctor came in and said,
"I really do not know how to tell you this.
That lump you that you found is indeed a mass.
I know this is not what you wanted to hear."

"The mammogram confirmed your discovery.
We will have to run further tests to see if it malignant.
Go out to the receptionist area
and reschedule an appointment for a biopsy.
Until the results are for sure, do not stress or increase your anxiety."

What! He just told me the lump I found in my breast is a mass!
I already had thoughts going through my my head,
but I was NOT to stress?
I did not get an appointment for another two weeks.
How did he suppose I keep this off my mind?
I could not just go sit in a beautiful meadow and meditate in the grass.

The biopsy verified that it was indeed cancer.
I was filled with so many emotions. I was sad, fearful,
And I felt lost and hopeless.
I thought my life as I knew it was over.
I was also relieved to finally have the answer.

I found out that it was in the early stages.
I had to have a bilateral mastectomy, with reconstructive surgery.
However, I was not bitter or sad. I got to live my life.
Breast Cancer is an evil villain,
it picks on men and women of all ages.

North Bound Railroad

A railroad with no train depots but made many stops.
She made it her life's work to be the conductor.
She first liberated herself.
She went back for her family, including her Mom and Pops.

Some may not know that she suffered from Narcolepsy
Or that her first husband would go, and remarry.
However she did not let this stop her.
Many do not even know that she was a spy for the Union Army.

She used code names and followed the stars,
Such as "Polaris" and "The North Star."
She always avoided capture.
She knew that would have been some nasty scars.

She led three hundred slaves to freedom.
Making over nineteen trips.
She was the "Conductor" also known as "Moses"
On the "Underground Railroad System."

NORTH AND SOUTH

I grew up in a military family so I have been to several different places.
I mostly lived in Indiana for about twenty years.
I consider this the North. I am going to compare
       Indiana (the North) to Florida (the South).
To me there are some reflecting differences.
       In both states one will see people of all faces.

In Indiana the police all have red and blue lights.
The volunteer firemen have lights of all blue.
This was a big adjustment for me when I relocated.
I had to figure this out quick, or they would have read me my rights!

The vast number of homeless, this is something
       that required some acclimation.
I had just moved from a place that had very few.
To a place that had them virtually everywhere.
The numbers literally quadrupled in this population.

I am still trying to get accustomed
       to the Southern dialects and inflections.
In the North people tend to talk really fast.
In the South people slow down their speech
       but they also leave out letters.
Such as when saying you are welcome it comes out as "You welcome."
At times, it is still really hard for me to comprehend these connections.

In the South the people believe in smiles and respect.
A person will often say "Thank you"
        and will open a door for a stranger.
They will smile at someone for no reason at all.
I have found that this does not discriminate to race, gender, or age.
People in the South are very personable and welcoming
        in the ways that they choose to connect.

A funeral progression, for me makes the biggest impact.
I love how in the South, the world comes to a complete stop.
For the one who just lost their life.
This shows the ultimate respect and in my eyes is a top rated class act.

"The Headless Horseman" Review

The dancers all had such precision and elegance,
As they danced across the stage.
Their bodies floated in an effortless motion.
Each one of them in sync, each with perfect balance.

I sat there absolutely still, I was hypnotized.
My eyes bounced back and forth to every ballerino and ballerina.
I did not want to miss any twirls or any leaps.
I was in awe, I was totally mesmerized.

They would start at balance and then they would end with en pointe.
I loved the single dancing as much as the partnering.
The duets had so much rhythm,
They worked so well together like that of a tongue and grove joint.

The whole ballet was greatly choreographed.
I loved how the scenery, the music, and the dance
all complemented each other.
The costumes added that much more to the story being told.
In my mind I will always have that particular ballet photographed.

Pensacola Ballet put on a program that was just magnificent.
That particular ballet will forever be with me.
I will recall it over and over again as time passes on.
That was a great night of more than entertainment.

To Reduce Life's Stress and Anxieties

Close your eyes to a visionary state; what is it that your mind sees?
Some may see the snow capped mountain peaks.
Some may see the tranquility of the blue oceans.
Others may see beautiful parks beneath the evergreen trees.

I see sunrises that are dazzling yellows.
Sunsets that are a blazing with crimson.
Rainbows that seem to have more pronounced indigos.
If you are feeling gray, picture this to take your sorrows away.

Listen to some instrumental music. I would recommend a soft piano.
Put on head phones, close your eyes, let the music move you,
Tune everything else out! Relax!
Let your body begin to sway to the music; you will follow.

Think about nothing but the music.
Listen to it, feel it, breathe with it.
Forgetting about everything else for a few moments of time.
Oh how it reduces Life's Stresses and anxieties. It's almost hypnotic.

Quiet the Mind, Quiet the Body

Is my life complete? Do I know how to love?
Do I really take the time to listen to the thoughts?
Do I really hear the music? Do I feel at peace?
Do I even know what I am in search of?

These are the questions that I am constantly asking myself.
I close my eyes, I am on a quest, and I am looking deep into my mind.
I see an extensive library of knowledge. My mind is full,
Yet, that one book I seek, is not on any shelf.

I can try to find these answers on someone's written page;
I am sure someone has written their own solutions to these uncertainties.
But with that, I will only find anxiety and frustration.
This is sure to only cause me internal rage.

To find true satisfaction I must look inside out.
However, when I look inside this is a noisy book store.
I think to myself there is no way I can pull out these answers.
I cannot see or hear anything. I get overwhelmed with doubt.
I need some solitude. I must quiet my mind.
I have to shut out some of this noise.
I have to have block it out.
There are answers that I seek, that I know I can now find.

I take some personal time, where nothing else matters.
The room gets quiet.
My mind and my body become calmer.
To my surprise, hidden inside, out came the answers.

Is my life complete? Yes, my life is complete.
Do I know how to love? Yes, I love myself so I can love others.
Do I really take the time to listen to the thoughts? Yes, my thoughts drive me.
Do I really hear the music? Yes, I can hear and feel the music. It moves me.
Do I feel at peace? Yes. For once in my life I am at peace.
Do I even know what I am in search of?
I was in search of that internal peace. That sense of calmness.

The Healing Bridge

I am healing, I am crossing the bridge from the darkness.
I am regaining control of my life. I am discovering who I am.
I know what I have done. I am learning I can no longer blame you.
I am yearning to live, love and to deal again. I am not worthless!

We all have done our share of wrong deeds.
I can only be accountable for my own actions,
I have to learn to forgive others for their actions,
For these actions, that I now know were not of my control.
I have to try and make amends and see where the road leads.

My accountability starts with self-forgiving.
Let me just say, this is not an easy task!
I have been quite the sinister, I have not been a saint!
There are still days where I still feel like, "Who am I kidding?!"

I can slowly feel the warmth of the love from inside my heart.
It is starting to pump through my frosty veins,
It is validating the hidden self-worth
That is helping me make this fresh new healing start.
I am hoping that with this new internal love that I am feeling,
I will be able to one day to project out of my beating heart,
towards others that have hurt me.
This will truly give me a complete sense of healing.

True Testament of Love at First Sight

The day his eyes saw hers, their lives changed forever.
He knew that soon they would be husband and wife.
He also knew that, he would be with her for a long time.
It was with that first look, he knew that he loved her.

This was a true testament of love at first sight.
She equally fell head over heels.
Soon they were together all the time.
To be so young and inseparable, together day and night.

Multiplied and divided was their love.
They had two beautiful children.
Then two amazing grandchildren.
Through good and bad times, he gave her a life she dreamed of.

Their life together has not always been the fairy tale story.
They have had their ups and downs,
They had their share of arguments and their fights.
After twenty-five years, they still have that loving glory.

Dancing in the Mist

The sky is gloomy, there is no sun to be found.
The moisture hovers densely in the air.
There is a peaceful breeze present.
I begin to look around.

Rain is falling in the form of a mist.
It is just enough to make one damp.
I smile to the sky,
On my face the water sprays. I can't resist.

Everyone else begins to dart inside.
I stand there for a moment.
Almost like I am in a trance.
Then I feel my love take my hand in his with pride.

He puts his arms around me and we begin to sway.
We do not care that others have stopped to watch.
We continue to dance.
It felt like we could dance the day away.

ALSO FROM ENERGION PUBLICATIONS

"I really enjoyed the process of writing this book and writing is always cheaper than counseling," says Lee Baker. "It's a good outlet for crazy people. In my life, crazy is in abundant supply."

ALSO BY TABITHA EDWARDS-WALTON

Just $9.99 direct from Energion Publications or available via on-line retailers.

More from Energion Publications

Personal Study
Finding My Way in Christianity	Herold Weiss	$16.99
The Jesus Paradigm	David Alan Black	$17.99

Christian Living
Faith in the Public Square	Robert D. Cornwall	$16.99
Grief: Finding the Candle of Light	Jody Neufeld	$8.99
Crossing the Street	Robert LaRochelle	$16.99
Surviving a Son's Suicide	Ron Higdon	$9.99

Bible Study
Learning and Living Scripture	Lentz/Neufeld	$12.99
When People Speak for God	Henry Neufeld	$17.99
Luke: A Participatory Study Guide	Geoffrey Lentz	$8.99
Philippians: A Participatory Study Guide	Bruce Epperly	$9.99
Ephesians: A Participatory Study Guide	Robert D. Cornwall	$9.99
Evidence for the Bible	Elgin Hushbeck, Jr.	

Theology
Creation in Scripture	Herold Weiss	$12.99
Creation: the Christian Doctrine	Edward W. H. Vick	$12.99
Creation in Contemporary Experience	David Moffett-Moore	$9.99
Ultimate Allegiance	Robert D. Cornwall	$9.99
Reframing a Relevant Faith	Drew Smith	$11.99
The Journey to the Undiscovered Country	William Powell Tuck	$9.99
The River of LIfe	Lee Harmon	$9.99
Process Theology	Bruce Epperly	$4.99

Ministry
Clergy Table Talk	Kent Ira Groff	$9.99
So Much Older Then …	Robert LaRochelle	$9.99
The Caregiver's Beatitudes	Robert Martin	$4.99
The Vicar of Tent Town	Shauna Hyde	$9.99

Generous Quantity Discounts Available
Dealer Inquiries Welcome
Energion Publications — P.O. Box 841
Gonzalez, FL 32560
Website: http://energionpubs.com
Phone: (850) 525-3916

www.ingramcontent.com/pod-product-compliance
Lightning Source LLC
Chambersburg PA
CBHW031614040426
42452CB00006B/515